All You Need Is Love

All You Need Is Love

an anthology of tanka on the Love of Life
with contributions from 62 Australian poets

edited by Amelia Fielden

All You Need is Love
ISBN 978 1 74027 918 5
Copyright © text individual poets 2015
Copyright © this collection Amelia Fielden 2015
Cover image by 'pling: Noriko Tadano performing in 'Noriko
& George' (George Kamikawa and Noriko Tadano) at the Nara
Candle Festival, 26 October 2013

First published 2015 by
GINNINDERRA PRESS
PO Box 3461 Port Adelaide SA Australia
www.ginninderrapress.com.au

Preface

When I sent out a call to my fellow Australian tanka writers for submissions on the theme of love, I emphasised that what I had in mind for this new anthology was tanka which would interpret the word 'love' in its broadest possible connotations, which would express and reflect each poet's 'love of life'.

In response, I received a wonderful variety of 'love' poetry which I am delighted to present here for your reading enjoyment.

Amelia Fielden MA

so much
to live for, she says
and shows me
the pot, its sweet pea seeds
soaking in the autumn rain

Saeko Ogi

chemistry cannot hide
my parting's silver
my passion now
for heirloom china
and my ageing cat

Judith Ahmed

my heartbeat
increases
on your mark…
my pride and joy
steps onto the podium

~~~~

a magpie choir
captures my morning
harmonies
of perfect pitch and tone…
again I am late for work

Bett Angel-Stawartz

I keep
living it over
late at night
after he stopped breathing
the softness of his fur

~~~~

every weekday
minding granddaughter
a mountain
of travel brochures stacked
under toys in the corner

~~~~

they say
the universe
is egg-shaped –
it lies in my garden
under a broken nest

Lynette Arden

first ultrasound
two tiny sacs pulse
…a pause
until my mind can name
what my eyes can see

~~~~

I bathe you
in a silvery basin
filled to the brim –
tiny fingers grasp my thumb
trace whorls upon my heart

~~~~

raining still,
Warragamba dam is full –
your songs
spill from the shower
into our lives

Anne Benjamin

a family
of crimson rosellas
in the native pine –
my upside-down
Christmas in July

~~~~

Latin lovers
serenade the suburbs
frogs and crickets
woo clotheslines
of moonlit lingerie

~~~~

letting go
of the past I wish I'd had
your hand in mine –
two glider possums
cross the winter moon

Michelle Brock

in the southerly
leaves tremble –
my mother's heart
is with my foundling magpie
during his first wild night

~~~~

drowned branches
of the drought-felled
river gum
once again alive…
a school of rainbows

~~~~

around her neck
shells and hag stones –
my hippy daughter
with love in the spring
of her step

Belinda Broughton

she reads
one tanka after another
to her lover…
the gentle pattering
of spring rain

~~~~

shakuhachi player…
the room fills
with notes
of such longing
strangers become friends

~~~~

fading sunset…
I drape a tartan rug
over his knees
and my arms
around his shoulders

Dawn Bruce

surprise!
a Valentine's Day card
in my mailbox
our forty-year friendship
turns a new page

Rhonda Byrne

    without you
    cluttering shelves
    such space
    in my library,
    between these ears

Penelope Cottier

unrequited
my lifetime hammock-longing,
never two trees
close enough to sling one
to enclose and nurture me

Jan Dean

        indulge me a while
        as I re-order my past
        and find you there –
        if suddenly I should wake
        just hold my hand in the present

Christopher Dorman

elephants trumpet
the matriarch thunders
herding the young
she corrals them to the centre –
a lion slinks past

Tess Driver

new tendrils
on climbing vines
reach out –
my heart lifts
in the early light

Maria Encarnacao

sunlight
ripples on the pond
flickers
over stone lanterns –
perhaps I love you still

~~~~

                bird etchings
                in the pale dawn skies
                of winter
                weeks and weeks
                until your probable return

Amelia Fielden

when I grow
too old to travel
my dreams
will take me back to Japan
in cherry blossom time

~~~~

        sixty-one years
        of cherished friendship
        remaining alive
        only in my memories
        the boy and man you were

RIP Michael

Amelia Fielden

lurching voices
on an Indian bus
'But he left his wife!'
'Love comes from God…'
I grasp the proffered handhold

~~~~

her dark locks
uncoiling under moonlight
Ganga* rushes by
…to a longed-for tryst
with the waiting plain

~~~~

moved by love†
to walk India's dust
to ask for land
for those with none …
his message strides on

Sylvia Florin

---

* Ganga is the Hindi and Sanskrit name for both the Ganges and its personifying goddess.

† *Moved by Love* is the title of an English translation of Vinoba Bhave's (1895–1982) memoirs.

your kiss
summons me from sleep
in the dark
beating heart of night
I hear drums…

Jan Foster

the choir sings
loving shepherd of thy sheep,
tears come to my eyes…
those childhood memories
of feeding motherless lambs

~~~~

new book published
by a favourite author
is advertised,
now on my shopping list
to share with friends

June Foster

her email keens
at the airport wifi lounge
where are you? come back –
he replies, stroking her neck,
internet kiss marks

~~~~

Sunday night ironing
my daughter's school tunic pleats
a labour of love
threading camels
through a needle's eye

~~~~

my brother rings
from five hundred miles away
in a storm
close to tears he asks
where will I sleep tonight

David Gilbey

feet to the floor
alarm bells ringing
rush to catch a train –
don't stand between me
and today's first cappuccino

~~~~

                    sun going down
                    and the white cat snoozing
                    on the worn brick wall
                    after half a lifetime
                    our love still holds its heat

Beverley George

movie music
releases me to other lives
in my kitchen
I stride like Katie Hepburn
tap-dance like Fred Astaire

~~~~

                    waking to the sound
                    of water falling on stones,
                    pale light through shoji
                    why do I feel so at home
                    in a country not my own

Beverley George

wild storm —
I hold her to my breast
stroke her hair
and feel the throb
of her purring

~~~~

in my garden
intricately woven
softly lined
this small storm-blown nest…
anguished cries from above

Margaret L. Grace

once he knelt
on a faded worn rug
loosely knotted
with wilting roses
and offered undying love

~~~~

                translucent
                persimmons light village lanes
                in the fall
                how can I say
                sayonara to this

Margaret L. Grace

this morning
a currawong came calling
left me a note
that told me
spring is nearly here

Jill Gower

the fresh sun
warms my metal mailbox,
the harsh frost
dripping down to running tears
while I wait for you to write

~~~~

caring for
is not the same as caring about
he complains –
why does he not understand
that if I didn't I couldn't

Janne Graham

coffee
or chocolate
for our muses –
boil the kettle,
Eros likes it hot

~~~~

a flight
of pink-breasted galahs
at day's end
my unpinned ribbon
rests by her photograph

Hazel Hall

approaching
headlights in the mist
dip over the hill
raising my hopes
it might be you

Simon Hanson

trees bask
in each other's reflections…
the bitter-sweet tears
of a camino ending,
emails exchanged at dawn

~~~~

                purple shadows
                cast petals across
                the path –
                your gifts of wisdom
                perennial in my heart

Carole Harrison

Bangarra dancer
on the Opera House stage
signals,
index finger outlining his heart
points to the girl in row A

~~~~

                 taking
                 the wave as it folds
                 judging
                 the exact moment to launch
                 between ocean and shoreline

Gail Hennessy

imprinted
on Turkish Roman pavement
a left foot
points the way
to the brothel

~~~~

        separated
        by a barbed wire fence
        two steers
        who used to be together,
        bellowing now at nightfall

Lorne Henry

seeing in colours
radiant from a simple smile
ever since that first kiss
an angel on the earth
a friend to lie beside

James Holcombe

she smiles
when the music starts
reliving
loved songs and dances
yesterday becomes today

Lois Holland

children's fingers
pollinate orchid to bean
vanilla…
taste of love
scent of sophistication

Andrew Howe

he places
a red rosebud
on her desk –
they exchange smiles
maybe, maybe this time

Marilyn Humbert

top of the range
candle heath in flower
and the scent
of alpine mint bush –
I wander in wonder

~~~~

                    dappled sunlight
                    under the plane tree
                    suddenly he's five
                    and the future quivers
                    in his dimpled smile

Gerry Jacobson

what if
mother had shared my love
for Beethoven
cadence after imperfect cadence,
would I play the blues less?

~~~~

                    brushing aside
                    memories of you
                    never works –
                    if I dust your photo
                    you smile even more

Kathy Kituai

I have found
when I take a lover
I lose earrings
but oh! the delight
of not searching for them

~~~~

        if Stevie Wonder
        calls to say I love you
        will I tremble
        the way I do when you phone
        and sing his words to me

Kathy Kituai

absorbed
into our family
already
this new puppy
this new start

~~~~

a chocolate
slowly melting
in my mouth –
I savour each moment
of this delicious affair

~~~~

never
one for dessert
until
you taught me how
to linger in anticipation

Keitha Keyes

plum blossom
pink among the gums
lone reminder
of a soldier's heart
broken by the land

~~~~

                blue felt hat
                high in the cupboard
                a fragment
                of you still remains
                after all these years

Kate King

a thousand stars
jump from ripple to ripple
across the lake
your headlights through the trees
coming home to me

Kate King

on that far island
among those soft, cloud-lit hills
you passed by unseen –
did I hear your farewell song
never lovers, ever friends

Jane Le Rossignol

joined at the breast
the heart and the gaze
of motherlove –
twenty-one on Wednesday
can't catch his eye

~~~~

        even her dog
        whose affection is
        unconditional
        detaches himself
        and moves away

Catherine McGrath

we sit quietly
how was your day?
full, and yours?
the same –
the mirror catches the light

Sue MacKenzie

gently held
in sea-hardened hands
a precious pearl,
cradled in his arms
a newborn daughter

Vyonne McLelland-Howe

five great-grandchildren
bury Taffy's ashes beneath
three rose trees –
we celebrate his life
free from pain at last

Marian Morgan

freesias
with fragile petals
musky scents
bring back those days
when I was by his side

Saeko Ogi

maternity ward
my minutes old son
suckling at my breast –
I never knew
there was love like this

~~~~

stretchmarks
proof that you
have changed me –
the rain-swollen river carves
a new channel to the sea

Vanessa Proctor

your skin is salt
delicate blue seagrass
undulating
above your ankle
a love tattoo ages with us

Sandra Renew

airport check-in
replete with bleached hair
and surfboards
the innocent sweetness
of holiday romance

~~~~

                              propelled
                              by the hot wind
                              a wild orchid
                              dances across the billabong
                              carefree as our first summer

Cynthia Rowe

old family home
where a generation grew
hugged by the walls –
walking through for the last time
her mother draws the curtains

Margaret Ruckert

your kiss
was it offered or taken?
– passion flowed
for a brief moment
the fruit tasted divine

Ken Sheerin

instinct tells
the old black labrador
to lay his head
upon her knee…he knows
her young heart is broken

~~~~

three cheers
for satellite navigation
in my car —
I never thought I could
love a bossy woman

Catherine Smith

treasures
to take on our bus ride
he grasps
a tiny suitcase
filled with small cars

Crys Smith

why do I dream
of far away shores…
still unmapped
the inner reaches
of my heart

~~~~

my daughter
stirs cinnamon and cloves
into sliced apples
the golden tang of pastry
my mother's recipe

~~~~

at my age
this second wind catches
my breath …
these fingers shy to trace
the long curve of your back

Carmel Summers

from peak to peak
each topped with a rosy tor,
my thirst for love
drives me across the downy plain
to drink at the mossy spring

Rupert Summerson

the moon
knitted with dreams
overflowing
with that old promise
of joy forever

Jill Sutton

crimson sunrise
…this lush valley
comes alive
with wolf whistles
from pied currawongs

~~~~

        my daily delights
        the flashy reds and greens
        of king parrots
        through the drooping white
        to gold of trumpet blooms

Barbara Taylor

making love only
weekends and birthdays
the labour
of colouring-in
between the lines

~~~~

                        darkness drops
                        like exhausted birds
                        of passage –
                        every day the silence
                        between us lengthens

David Terelinck

'for lease' signs
in empty windows –
does anyone
really know why
they fall out of love

~~~~

                        the scrimshaw
                        of those who have never
                        been to sea…
                        men who can tattoo
                        'I love you' to the bone

David Terelinck

posted west
to ironbark country,
will their young love
grow just as hardy
flower just as red?

~~~~

                I lust
                for your slender limbs
                your soft tresses
                and your perfume at night,
                lemon-scented gum

Michael Thorley

we dined
beside the Opera House
the Bridge
and the harbour lights –
saw only each other

~~~~

        an old couple
        sitting on a street bench
        side by side
        their smart phones giving them
        someone to talk to

Michael Thorley

mere children
on the day we married
we poured
free champagne
down the hotel sink

~~~~

                    plane trees
                    drop their first leaves
                    on this lamplit avenue
                    you take my hand
                    as we walk the storm-cleansed path

Julie Thorndyke

don't they say
out of sight, out of mind
if you are gone
why can't I learn
the art of forgetting

~~~~

        journal pages
        of dense black text –
        I begin
        to think of you
        in the past tense

Julie Thorndyke

whoever thought
books might disappear
into cyberspace?
safe in bookshelves mine wait
their turn to be caressed

Jo Tregellis

a friend's sudden death —
at our last parting
just three weeks back
if only I'd stayed to share
the glass of wine he offered

Lesley Walter

I love you
echoing through the valley
you you you
tell me how, tell me why
why why why…

~~~~

        in tennis
        love is the score of nil –
        love all
        in life and in tennis
        gives us chances to serve

Ellen Weston

my offering
to the satin bowerbird
a blue clothes peg
to enhance his eligibility
with the ladies of the bush

Joanne Watcyn-Jones

stiff with sheen
creaking as we stretch,
straight off the shelf
a brand new pair of shoes
yet to break each other in

~~~~

winter moon
one night shy of full…
that blink
of hesitation
before her reassurance

Rodney Williams

flying visit
grandmother is smitten
with baby,
her dark curls
her connecting smile

Paul Williamson

as we join hands
in a groundswell of fervour
I'm overwhelmed
by the light in their eyes
and the warmth in their hearts

Beatrice Yell

every morning
a small white dog
runs to the shore
and barks at the frothy waves
that swallowed its master

~~~~

        one day
        in a future life
        you and I
        will make our journey
        on the wings of a butterfly

Athena Zaknic

Authors

Judith Ahmed	7	Lois Holland	30
Bett Angel-Stawartz	7	Andrew Howe	31
Lynette Arden	8	Marilyn Humbert	31
Anne Benjamin	9	Gerry Jacobson	32
Michelle Brock	10	Kathy Kituai	33–34
Belinda Broughton	11	Keitha Keyes	35
Dawn Bruce	12	Kate King	36–37
Rhonda Byrne	13	Jane Le Rossignol	37
Penelope Cottier	13	Catherine McGrath	38
Jan Dean	14	Sue MacKenzie	39
Christopher Dorman	14	Vyonne McLelland-Howe	39
Tess Driver	15	Marian Morgan	40
Maria Encarnacao	15	Saeko Ogi	40
Amelia Fielden	16–17	Vanessa Proctor	41
Sylvia Florin	18	Sandra Renew	41
Jan Foster	19	Cynthia Rowe	42
June Foster	19	Margaret Ruckert	43
David Gilbey	20	Ken Sheerin	43
Beverley George	21–22	Catherine Smith	44
Margaret L. Grace	23–24	Crys Smith	44
Jill Gower	25	Carmel Summers	45
Janne Graham	25	Rupert Summerson	46
Hazel Hall	26	Jill Sutton	46
Simon Hanson	26	Barbara Taylor	47
Carole Harrison	27	David Terelinck	48–49
Gail Hennessy	28	Michael Thorley	50–51
Lorne Henry	29	Julie Thorndyke	52–53
James Holcombe	30	Jo Tregellis	54

Lesley Walter	54	Paul Williamson	57
Ellen Weston	55	Beatrice Yell	57
Joanne Watcyn-Jones	56	Athena Zaknic	58
Rodney Williams	56		

Acknowledgements

Some of these tanka have been previously published as follows:

Ahmed, Judith: chemistry cannot hide, *Eucalypt: a tanka journal*, ed. Beverley George, Australia, issue 13, 2012

Brock, Michelle: Latin lovers, *Atlas Poetica, Tanka of Urban Life*, ed. M. Kei, USA, 2013

Broughton, Belinda: around her neck, *Bright Stars, An Organic Tanka Anthology*, ed. M. Kei, USA, vol. 2, 2014

Fielden, Amelia: bird etchings, *Baubles, Bangles & Beads*, Amelia Fielden, Ginninderra Press, Australia, 2007

George, Beverley: feet to the floor, *The Tanka Journal*, ed. Aya Yuhki, Japan, no. 39, 2011

—: sun going down, *red lights*, ed. Marilyn Hazelton, USA, vol. 3 no. 2, 2007

—: waking to the sound *Poetry Nippon*, third series, edition no. 2, The Poetry of Japan, Japan, 2011

Hall, Hazel: a flight, *Moonbathing: a journal of women's tanka*, ed. Pamela A. Babusci, USA, issue 10, 2014

Hanson, Simon: approaching, *GUSTS: Contemporary Tanka*, ed. Kozue Uzawa, Canada, no. 19, 2014

Jacobson, Gerry: dappled sunlight, *GUSTS*, op. cit., no. 20, 2014

Kituai, Kathy: brushing aside, and I have found, *In Two Minds*, Amelia Fielden & Kathy Kituai, Modern English Tanka Press, USA, 2008

—: Stevie Wonder, and what if, *Yesterday, Today & Tomorrow*, Amelia Fielden & Kathy Kituai, Interactive Press, Australia, 2011

Ogi, Saeko: so much, *Eucalypt*, op. cit., issue 16, 2014

Proctor, Vanessa: maternity ward, and stretchmarks, *Presence*, ed. Martin Lucas, UK, no. 28, 2005

Rowe, Cynthia: propelled, *paper wasp: a journal of haiku*, ed. Katherine Samuelwitz, Australia, vol. 17, no. 2, 2011

Sheerin, Ken: your kiss, *Koi*, Ken Sheerin, armchair publishing, Australia, 2014

Summers, Carmel: at my age, *GUSTS*, op. cit., no. 15, 2012

Terelinck, David: making love, *Ribbons: Tanka Society of America Journal*, ed. David Rice, USA, vol. 9, no. 2, 2013

—: darkness drops, *The Tanka Journal*, op. cit., no.45, 2014

—: 'for lease' signs, *GUSTS*, op. cit., no. 20, 2014

—: the scrimshaw, First place, tanka section, 2013 British Haiku Awards; *Blithe Spirit*, ed. David Bingham, UK, vol. 24, no. 2, 2014

Thorndyke, Julie: don't they say, *Carving Granite*, Julie Thorndyke, Ginninderra Press, Australia, 2011

—: journal pages, *Rick Rack*, Julie Thorndyke, Ginninderra Press, Australia, 2008

Williams, Rodney: stiff with sheen and winter moon, *A Bird-Loving Man*, Rodney Williams, Ginninderra Press, Australia, 2013

www.ingramcontent.com/pod-product-compliance
Lightning Source LLC
Chambersburg PA
CBHW062201100526
44589CB00014B/1895